PIANO · VOCAL · GUITAR

2013 GREATEST CHRISTIAN Hits

2013

★SHEET MUSIC for the Year's Most Popular Songs★
★DELUXE ANNUAL EDITION★

D1305889

Alfred

Produced by
Alfred Music Publishing Co., Inc.
P.O. Box 10003
Van Nuys, CA 91410-0003
alfred.com

Printed in USA.

ISBN-10: 0-7390-9602-8
ISBN-13: 978-0-7390-9602-4

Cover Photo
Concert Crowd: © istockphoto / miappv

 Alfred Cares. Contents printed on 100% recycled paper.

CONTENTS

10,000 Reasons
(Bless the Lord)

Words and Music by
MATT REDMAN and JONAS MYRIN

Slow worship ballad ♩ = 72

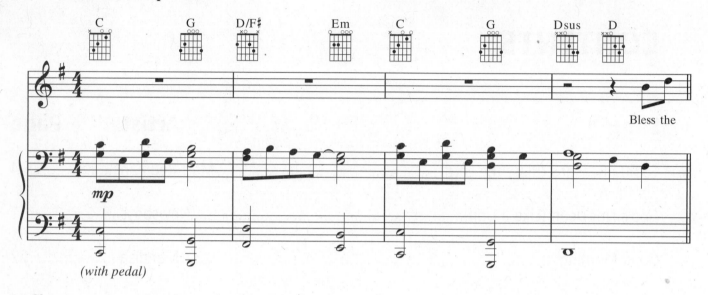

(with pedal)

Chorus:

Verse 3:

on that day when my strength is fail - ing, the end draws near and my

time has come,___ still my soul will sing Your___ praise un -

end - ing,___ *(drum)* ten thou - sand years and then for -

ev - er - more. Bless the

mf

GOD'S NOT DEAD (Like a Lion)

Words and Music by
DANIEL BASHTA

Verse 3:

lost in___ Your___ free - dom,___

and this world___ I'll o - ver -
Ah.___

come.___ My God's___ not dead, He's sure - ly a - lieve.__ He's liv -

Chorus:

ing on the in - side, roar-ing like a li - on. God's not dead, He's

N.C.
Em7
G♯m7
D
F♯
roar-ing like a li - on. Roar - ing, He's roar - ing, He's roar-
G
B
Em7
G♯m7
ing like a li - on. He's roar - ing, He's roar-
D
F♯
G
B
Roar - ing like a li - on.
ing, He's roar - ing like a li - on.
Em7
G♯m7
D
F♯
G
B
mp

GOOD MORNING

Words and Music by
AARON RICE, CARY BARLOWE, JAMIE MOORE,
MANDISA HUNDLEY and TOBY MCKEEHAN

Café au lait, latte dah. You do the zumba, but I do not.   Give me like half a marathon, I'll

give you the Gospel of St. John. Hits me like a wake up bomb, 'cuz we both know that's His mercy flows in the

Chorus:

morn-ing.___   This   morn - ing.___

mornin'.   Wake up to a brand new___ day.___   I'm   step-ping, step-ping,

HOLD ME

Words and Music by
CHRIS STEVENS, JAMIE GRACE
and TOBY McKEEHAN

Moderately bright reggae feel ♩ = 136

I love, I love, I love, I love the way You hold__ me.

I love, I love, I love, I love the way You hold__ me. I love, I love, I love, I

love the way You hold__ me. I love, I love, I love, I love the way You, the way You...

* Guitar capo at 4th fret.

Hold Me - 8 - 1

Verse 1 (sing first time only):

Verse 2 (sing second time only):

world is gon - na bring me down,   that's when Your smile comes a - round. Ooh,   I love the way You

fig - ure You out,___   You make me wan - na sing and shout.   I love the way You

Chorus:

hold me.   By___ my side You'll al - ways be. You take each and ev - 'ry day, make it spe - cial in___

___ some way. I love the way You hold me.   In___ Your arms I'll al - ways be. You take each and ev -

Chorus:

HOW GREAT IS OUR GOD

Words and Music by
JESSE REEVES, CHRIS TOMLIN
and ED CASH

Moderately slow acoustic rock ♩ = 76

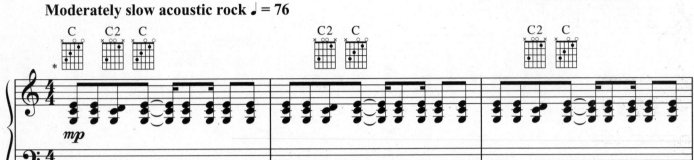

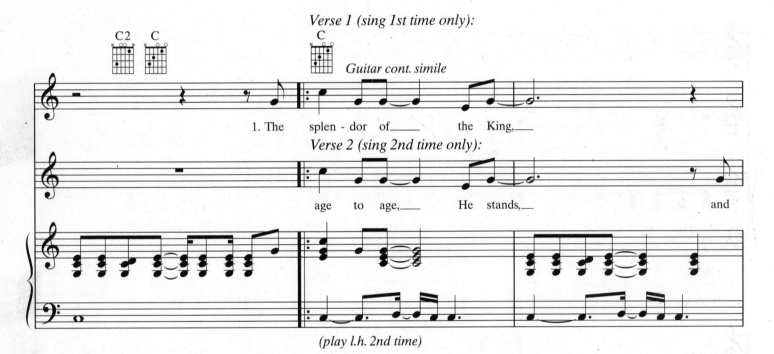

Verse 1 (sing 1st time only):

1. The splen-dor of___ the King,___

Verse 2 (sing 2nd time only):

age to age,___ He stands,___ and

(play l.h. 2nd time)

clothed in maj - es - ty;___ let all the earth_ re-joice,___ all the earth_ re-joice.___

time is in___ His hands;___ Be-gin-ning and_ the End,___ Be-gin-ning and_ the End._

*Original recording in D♭ major with Guitar Capo 1.

How Great Is Our God - 4 - 1

I NEED A MIRACLE

Words and Music by
DAVID CARR, MAC POWELL,
MARK LEE and TAI ANDERSON

Verse 1:

1. Well, late___ one night,___ she start - ed to cry and thought,___ ___ "He ain't com - in' home."___ She was tired___ of the lies, tired_ of the fight, but she

I Need A Miracle - 8 - 4

49

JESUS, FRIEND OF SINNERS

Words and Music by
MATTHEW WEST and MARK HALL

Jesus, Friend of Sinners - 10 - 1

Chorus:

54

Chorus:

56

rea-son that_You came. Lord, I was that lost cause,   and I was that out - cast,_   but You died for
(rea-son that_You came._____   I was that lost   cause,_____   and I was the out - cast._)

sin-ners just_ like_ me,_   a grate-ful lep-er at_ Your feet.___   'Cause You are_

good,   You are_ good,__   and Your love   en - dures for-

good, You are good. You are good. and Your love en-dures for-

Chorus:

ev-er. Je - sus, Friend of sin-ners, o-pen our eyes

to the world at the end of our point-ing fin - gers. let our hearts be led by

NEED YOU NOW (HOW MANY TIMES)

Words and Music by
CHRISTA WELLS, LUKE SHEETS
and TIFFANY ARBUCKLE

Slow pop groove ♩ = 66

(with pedal)

Verse 1:

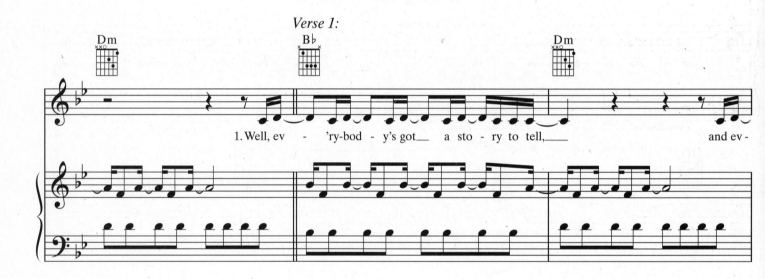

1. Well, ev - 'ry-bod - y's got___ a sto - ry to tell,___ and ev -

'ry - bod - y's got___ a wound___ to be healed.___ I want to be -

Need You Now - 6 - 1

Bridge:

ONE THING REMAINS

(Your Love Never Fails)

Words and Music by
JEREMY RIDDLE, BRIAN JOHNSON
and CHRISTA BLACK

THE PROOF OF YOUR LOVE

Words and Music by
LUKE SMALLBONE, JOEL DAVID SMALLBONE,
BEN GLOVER, FREDERICK WILLIAMS,
JONATHAN LEE, and MIA FIELDES

The Proof of Your Love - 6 - 1

REDEEMED

Words and Music by
BENJI COWART and MICHAEL WEAVER

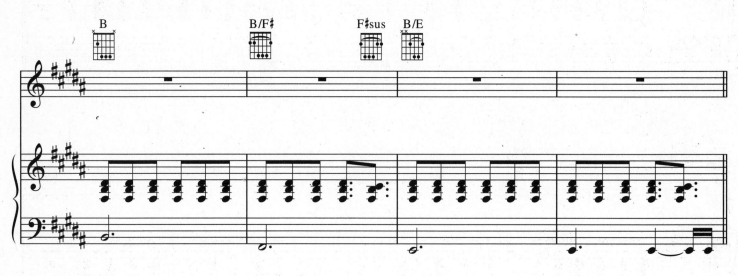

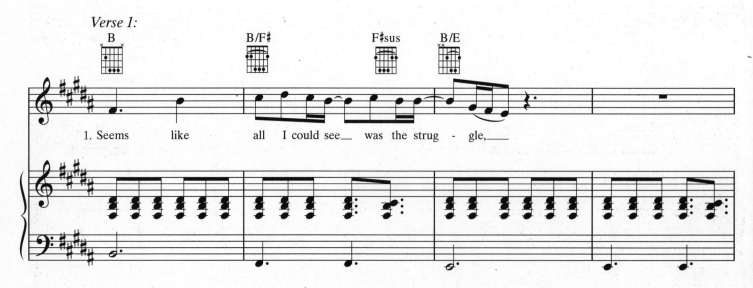

Verse 1:

1. Seems like all I could see__ was the strug - gle,__

Verse 2:

2. All my life I have been called un-wor-thy,

named by the voice of my shame and re-gret.

But when I hear You whis-per, "Child, lift up your head," I re-

mem-ber, O God, You're not done with me yet. I am re-

WE ARE

Words and Music by
ED CASH, CHUCK BUTLER,
JAMES TEALY and HILLARY McBRIDE

We Are - 7 - 1

88

We are chil - dren of____ the day.____ So

wake up, sleep - er, lift____ your head.__ We were meant_ for more___ than this.__

Fight the shad - ows, con - quer death,_ make the most_ of the time___ we have_ left.

Chorus:

We are the light of the world.__ We are the cit - y on a hill.___

WHO YOU ARE

Words and Music by
JASON WALKER, MICHAEL GOMEZ,
CHAD MATTSON and JON LOWRY

Chorus:

WHOM SHALL I FEAR
(GOD OF ANGEL ARMIES)

Words and Music by
CHRIS TOMLIN, ED CASH
and SCOTT CASH

Moderately slow rock ♩ = 75

*On the original recording, acoustic guitars play with capo 5.

Whom Shall I Fear (God of Angel Armies) - 7 - 1

YOU ARE

Words and Music by
RHYAN SHIRLEY, JARED MARTIN,
COLTON DIXON and MIKE BUSBEE

You Are - 7 - 1

YOUR LOVE NEVER FAILS

Words and Music by
ANTHONY SKINNER and CHRIS McCLARNEY